REFLECTIONS FROM OUR BREAKTHROUGHS

TAKING OWNERSHIP OF THE TRANSFORMATION

By

RONEIKO D. HENDERSON, LCSW

Copyright © 2023

Reflections By Roneiko

All rights reserved

Disclaimer

Although the author and the publisher have tried to ensure that the information in this book was correct at the press time, the author and publisher do not assume and disclaim any liability to any part for any loss, damage, or disruption caused by errors or omissions, whether such errors or omissions result from negligence, accident, or any other cause

I dedicate this book to my Reiki Master teacher Jose, what a road we have traveled, my dear friend. I thank you for not giving up on me and pushing me to see outside the box, that had me stuck in so many ways for so many years. You knew the assignment as soon as we met in this lifetime, and you assisted me with completing it, and I am forever grateful to you. You will always be my earth angel, my brother, and my dear friend for eternity.

To my mother, there are no words to thank you for every tear you have shared with and without me, every hurt you have watched me endure. God knew what he was doing when he granted me you as my mother. This journey has been a hell of a ride, and I am so glad I had you here in my corner. Know that I sincerely appreciate the lessons of strength learned within this season. I love you, Debra Faye.

To my son Wendell, what a journey this has been for us both. We were placed into transformational portals that prepared us for our start overs. Thank you for the lessons, wake-up calls, and love showered upon me. You are such a breath of fresh air to my soul, and I am beyond grateful for our bond. Your acceptance of me, despite my flaws, has been everything I need to push through. I love you times infinity and beyond.

Table of Contents

INTRODUCTION 6
NEW JOURNEY 7
EXPECTATIONS 10
FRIENDSHIP EXCHANGE 13
A FILLED CUP 16
CIGARS, SUNSET AND R&B 19
DARK 22
AFFIRMATIONS 25
REIKI 28
EMPTY NESTER REALIZATION 32
CHANGE OF VISION 36
THE GREAT PRETENDER 39
SOCIETAL ACCEPTANCE 42
MENTAL HEALTH 45
UNCLE MONK 48
RUNNING 51
MESSAGES 54
TRANSITIONS AND TRANSFORMATIONS 57
PEACE 61
VULNERABILITY 64

WHY	67
HER NEIKO	70
MIND, BODY, SPIRIT	73
DEBRA FAYE	76
RELEASING AND HEALING	80
BROTHERS AND SISTERS	83
SEASONAL	86
STARTING SOMETHING NEW	89
A NEW MEANING OF LOVE	93
REINTRODUCTION	96

INTRODUCTION

After returning to the States after living aboard, I faced my personal Pandemic. I knew it was time for me to do the inevitable, it was time to terminate relationships in my life, and there were so many components associated with these relationships that I was not prepared for all the turbulence I would encounter.

As a clinician, I thought I got this. However, that was not the case. Life has a funny way of teaching you valuable, sustainable lessons. Throughout this journey, I have been pulled in several directions. I must admit that my journey allowed me to grow mentally, spiritually, emotionally, and physically. It was mind-blowing for my mind, body, and spirit.

As I reread the chapters of *Thought Provoking Reflections During A Pandemic*, I knew there needed to be a follow-up about our thoughts on those breakthroughs we all have made.

As you read through *Reflections From Our Breakthroughs*, you can reflect on the breakthroughs that not only I have experienced, but those like yourself have experienced during the Pandemic and life, including job loss, death, divorce, depression, marriage, rebirth, and self-love. Although many may consider the Pandemic a time of strict grief and loss, there has been a sense of rebirth for many individuals and families. Our comeback from the rebirth will be the story within the story. Let's go.

"Do not conform to the pattern of this world, but be transformed by the renewing of your mind."

Romans 12:2 NIV

NEW JOURNEY

Within life, we come across many metaphors. A prevalent metaphor is the journey of life. Each journey is individualized and explicit. I have discovered upon my journey we are all on a mission. Who will ultimately judge our failures and success along the journey?

My journey exposed me to several twists and turns, mountains, peaks, and valleys throughout the pandemic. In addition, I have recognized some similarities as I consulted with others on marriage, children, employment, and figuring out what is next to discover complete happiness. Individually, this process has brought forth an array of emotions that have left some depressed, unmotivated, and stagnated. While others became motivated, inspired, examined new interests and hobbies, and removed themselves from relationships that no longer served their best interest.

The discoveries revealed during this life journey aren't an easy carrousel ride if we are honest with ourselves. It's a rollercoaster that will bring forth some deep soul-searching and truth of self. It isn't for the meek because you will confront some dark days. However, there are lights at the end of the tunnel.

Most individuals start a new journey in fear of failure. They have talked themselves out of what could be due to their subconscious thoughts of what will not be.

I have ascertained this journey of life provides ample possibilities. So our thoughts are imperative when beginning new unknown journeys. You have what it takes to succeed in this new journey.

> *"Go ahead and open the door; you will be surprised at what awaits you on this new journey, success, happiness, love, and peace."*

Reflections, Thoughts, Breakthroughs

EXPECTATIONS

Life has a funny way of playing tricks on your mind and heart with those you care about. We want to believe in the best intention of those that we love and cherish. However, there comes a time when even those individuals we love and cherish will disappoint or fall short of our expectations.

I once had someone tell me I should never place expectations upon humans because they will not hold up their end of the bargain. That was a harsh statement until I began to somewhat psychoanalysis the statement in general. I discovered that through living life, there would be ups and downs and several disappointments from life in general. However, does the individual in whom you place expectations know your expectations?

I do my best not to place individuals in a paradigm. However, I have discovered over the years that I generally place minimal expectations upon individuals. Perhaps, it is due to personal experience or not wanting to be let down. We all have faults, flaws, inconsistencies, and shortcomings. Some may come all within one day. Who am I to let my expectations dictate the intentions of an individual due to the feelings implemented upon my mind or heart?

"There must be mutual expectations to complete the paradigm."

Reflections, Thoughts, Breakthroughs

FRIENDSHIP EXCHANGE

We search for friendship outside our genetic bond with our siblings or cousins as a child. These relationships we sought explained the different personality traits of the human species and assisted us with developing our social skills, learning practical negotiation skills, handling rejection, and effective communication. Honestly, there are many emotions regarding the relationship exchange with our friends in our youth and adulthood.

When I hear the word friend, I always think of the hit song by Whodini in the 1980s. The lyrics are so profound and genuine. We discover a friend's true meaning through trial and error throughout life. Without thought, the echoed word will reveal a sense of inclusion; it isn't about quantity but quality.

As a clinician, I have told my clients that once they reach a certain age, they will discover that you will only need to use one hand to count their real ride-or-die friends in this life. I make the analogy by asking how many fingers you have on one hand. I always get a stunning look with the answer five. I reply we have three fingers, an index, a middle, and a pointer finger. The other two extremities on our hand are a thumb and a pinkie. The looks and laughs I received after that were mind-blowing.

We exercise so much energy to reach that perfect friend who will accept us for who we are and love us despite our flaws. So many experience problems building substantial friendships as adults. Take an honest inventory of your current friend list. Are you yoked, is the exchange equally distributed? Genuine friendship does not require quantity in numbers. It's the quality of the relationship exchange that wins every time.

"Grateful for my small circle of friends that have supported me through the good, bad, and ugly; thank you for your unconditional love."

Reflections, Thoughts, Breakthroughs

A FILLED CUP

All the new craze as we explore the meaning of the new phenomenon of "self-care." It is now a staple of many, yet a bad word for some to speak aloud. Our society has programmed us to feel some way if we dare to speak openly about caring for ourselves. Believing that assuring those around you were good would bring you the happiness you needed and or desired to fill your cup was a misconception provided. I had to reevaluate the idea of taking care of others before taking care of myself because I felt highly depleted. Often, my cup had reached complete emptiness.

Don't get me wrong; you must fill your cup to ensure you are functioning in alignment to be productive. Nourishing yourself can come with a price when others look at it.

As a mother, social worker, friend, and overall nurturing individual, I had focused on ensuring those within my immediate circle cups were always full because I wanted them to be happy. I was receptive to completing whatever it required of me to do that. I should have recognized that many individuals I poured into did not care about my cup's capacity. People will take as much as you allow them to and reciprocate nothing in return if you do not require them to do so. Throughout my travels, I discovered in some countries; it is customary to fill your cup first and then fill the cups of those around you. Incorporating this custom into my life has been fulfilling.

> *"Allow yourself to recognize the signs of becoming depleted and supply yourself with all the self-care needed to place your cup back to the brim."*

Reflections, Thoughts, Breakthroughs

CIGARS, SUNSET AND R&B

Today was a day of celebration from the moment I opened my eyes until I closed them to return to slumber. During several monumental moments, I was pulled to check in on a dear friend who has been a light on my path. I couldn't shake the feeling we needed to connect on this day. I followed my intuition, and we planned to meet on her side of town for a catch-up day. As soon as I looked at her, I knew I was exactly where I needed to be to provide the support and listening ear needed during this check-in catch-up day.

It is essential to follow those intuitions when it involves checking in on those individuals you are connected with. It was one of the in-depth conversations we have shared over the years we have been connected. I love we can always be transparent and vulnerable amongst one another and know that we are safe with our disclosures.

Society has misled us into believing we must withhold our inner feelings and emotions and share only the strength we process. Many have discovered this stance doesn't let us release what needs to be shared and expanded upon as it relates to our inner healing and clarification in retrospect to those innermost feelings and emotions. After a delicious brunch and dialogue, we had the opportunity to enjoy the sunset and water and a great cigar aligned with some ole school R&B to set the mood.

As our phenomenal day ended, we had the opportunity to converse with a couple walking by, enjoying the scenery. We found ourselves amongst fellow souls meant to cross paths with one another. Our hearts were overflowing as we shared the gifts of our souls. We each left with a new sense of clarity and celebration, knowing that everything on this day was especially completed in the order it was meant to happen.

"Follow those intuitions and see the story unfold before you."

Reflections, Thoughts, Breakthroughs

DARK

During a trip to Laos with my son, we visited excellent sightseeing excursions. I recall the beauty of Buddha Park. The park displayed many Hindu and Buddhist spiritual and symbolic artifacts. However, the most prominent sculpture in the park was different and intriguing. It stood tall and within the center of the park. Curiosity intrigued me as we approached, and I was eager to learn more about the gigantic figure.

The translator advised us that this replicates what many believe is the portal to heaven. Everyone proceeds to an immensely dark place to work out their darkness and sins committed on earth, and then you must work your way up to each level to reach heaven, was the explanation provided. After entering the sculpture, you are immediately greeted by the remains of skeleton bones and darkness on the first floor.

I thought deeply about the words provided by the translator. Growing up, I recall versions like Laos. So, what exactly is darkness? Webster's dictionary defines dark as "a place or time of little or no light."

Most people I have encountered do not like to discuss their sins committed or speak about their visit to the dark side of life. However, as a psychotherapist, I have met several individuals who defined their life outside of being perfect as entering life's dark side or darkness. I am astonished by the translation provided by humans for defining darkness. Many will correlate it on a religious spectrum, while others define it as something that only a few individuals will experience due to the impediments of drug use.

I beg to differ because we all wrestle with our darkness. But unfortunately, we avoid being in touch with our authentic shadow self, avoiding the work required to find the needed light.

"Darkness can provide light if you are open to letting it in."

Reflections, Thoughts, Breakthroughs

AFFIRMATIONS

I have had the opportunity to encourage individuals to use positive affirmations for many years. That face-to-face with self lets individuals speak for themself, reaffirming their ability to transpire or produce what is needed. However, it's an exciting concept challenging to master if you have been told all your life you cannot or will not be this or that by those you love or society. Unfortunately, many have missed out on providing themselves with self-love and positive affirmations due to ongoing negative self-talk and self-doubt.

When you scroll through social media outlets, you see that affirming oneself is the season's fashion. Some will say, what affirmations should I speak to myself for reassurance? What reassurance do you need to be identified and manifested at this very moment? Humans are great at placing blame and repeating ongoing negative messages throughout our silent head chat/thoughts. Even the most secure individual who projects a solid foundational aura outwardly has negative thoughts internally due to what they have heard and feel society needs them to project.

When it is all said, remember that you matter, and you can be and do whatever you set your mind to doing or being.

"A few solid affirmations will take you far; try it."

Reflections, Thoughts, Breakthroughs

REIKI

Back in 2012, after the transition of my father, I explored Reiki, meditation, and my spiritual journey. Unfortunately, it was short-lived because I had other obligations and goals I had set that needed to be met with more urgency, at least I thought. In addition, I had placed aside many connections to the explored journey externally rather than internally as I would soon discover.

Upon my return to the States after living in Asia to prepare my son for his college journey, I connected with my earth angel and brother for lunch and a long overdue catch-up. For some unknown reason, I knew I needed to reconnect with him as I was about to undergo one of the most transformations in my life. I felt his worry and knew I could no longer pretend I was okay. When I looked into his eyes, I knew that he knew I needed some assistance with this journey I was about to embark upon, not realizing how difficult it would be because I had convinced myself that I had it covered. I received the reassuring words I needed and knew I had support from my dear friend to aid me.

I traveled back to Asia to prepare for my final return to the States to take care of my affairs, heal all ailments, and accept my role in my life. During my time back in Korea, I did some soul-searching and some releasing, not clearly understanding I had a war to fight upon my return, and I needed to be ready for the fight of my life if I was to be victorious.

Upon my return, I provided my teacher with mental and physical health updates. I was losing a pound a day, and I had not accepted the toll this transformation took upon my entire being. I thought I got this, but I did not have it; I needed to accept that I needed to process all the emotions associated and release them. So, I used journaling to release and lots of crying, which can be very cleansing.

On top of all that I was enduring, I discovered that my son was not in a great place, further diverting my already frail disposition. So here I was, without answers nor the ability to soothe the person who meant so much in distress. I understood what I was groping with the return from Asia and the transition amongst me and how it affected me; now, I did not consider how the move and the transitions would affect him. It's amusing how our thoughts will place us in overdrive that will have us second-guessing everything. Did I make the right choice on returning, or should I continue to accept things and suck it up?

Upon my final return, we worked on securing the role our creator had explicitly created just for me. There are no words to describe that back-and-forth emotional rollercoaster I endured. My teacher gave me the truth throughout the ride and held me accountable for my actions, leaving no room for victimhood. I appreciate how he kept me on track to meet the goals established.

"Sometimes in life, when we feel lost, we simply need to do the work to find ourselves."

Reflections, Thoughts, Breakthroughs

EMPTY NESTER REALIZATION

Today as I ponder within my inner thoughts, watching the birds fly in the sky, enjoying every part of their being, I was hit with some deep emotions, and the tears flowed like a water faucet. I would no longer have the one constant that has always been in my life or within my reach for the first time in twenty years. I must admit that the past year has been an array of emotions, transformations, and healing. My life for the last 23 years ended through the termination of a marriage. Now, that within itself required some deep inner work. However, the one thing that represented an attachment to that union I once shared with my ex-husband was our son, and now it was time to allow him to depart and explore his journey independently. Wow, I thought I was ready for this, only to discover that I needed to go and do more internal work to address my emotions associated. Why was it hard for me to digest the inevitable? I knew he would be great at whatever path he chose.

When we become parents, we have many dreams for our children and want to protect them from obstacles in this life. We watch them go through the stages of development and enjoy figuring out what traits come from whom. Their personality and other elements shape them into the unique individual they are in this lifetime. Through my journey as a parent, I thought I had adequately prepared myself for the day my son would head off to college, knowing I would at least see him on holidays and breaks. Unbeknown to the fact that there would be a change in plans. Due to his change in plans, I may get a holiday occasionally. I immediately went to my feelings as I needed to process them and why they hit so hard. Realizing that his change was critical in my transformational growth, taking place internally and externally.

Here I was, a seasoned mother of one son, no longer in a committed marital relationship, discovering that the big start-over was happening and that I would be okay when it was all said and done. I am grateful for the journey I embarked upon with my son and know our bond will forever be embedded. I am proud of his choice as he embarks upon his new journey and explores all the opportunities and doors that await him.

As I return my gaze to the sky above, I see two birds flying high, enjoying their visit/time together. I recall they went in separate directions as they left, knowing each would be great on their new journey. What an epiphany provided as I am now an empty nester, knowing that my once little boy, now a man, is soaring like the King he inherited through birth.

"Laying the foundation for a great take-off is essential for our children to succeed."

Reflections, Thoughts, Breakthroughs

CHANGE OF VISION

I have discovered that my eyes aren't as great as they were in my younger days. However, those inexpensive reading glasses I prescribed were no longer getting the job done, so it was time to take the big plunge and head to the ophthalmologist for a thorough examination.

As I look toward a new journey, my sight has been blinded and the clearest that I can remember, if that makes sense. Going through life with blinders and not knowing what is right before you to receive clarity has been an intense journey. The illusions of people, places, and things are simultaneously so powerful and deadly. The exciting thing about those illusions is that no ophthalmologist can detect the clarity you seek within those illusions. The clarity we are seeking comes from within. I understood that it requires some shadow work that can be highly dark with no light in sight. However, there is light at the end of that tunnel we will come through.

As I received the results of my eye examination, there was no surprise I needed reading glasses negligibly more muscular than what I had been wearing. I translated the results received both externally and internally. Change is forever revolving in this game of life. What is required for us to experience expanded sight for understanding, confirmation, and clarity on a new spectrum of vision requires an open mind and acceptance of our destiny.

"Are you ready to see into a new dimension?"

Reflections, Thoughts, Breakthroughs

THE GREAT PRETENDER

On November 22, 1987, I crossed the burning sands of the illustrious Delta Sigma Theta Sorority, Incorporated, Alpha Chi Chapter Tennessee State University. I was given the line name "Great Pretender." I tried to figure out how the big sisters came up with such a name, as did my line sisters with their names provided, but I let it go and kept it moving.

Little did I discern the name suited me at that moment. Only a couple of my big sisters knew of some family perplexities I was undertaking during my pledging process that would have caused others to perhaps drop the line, but I continued to persevere. I professed that all was well, although my world was crumbling.

I do that more than I would like to admit. It became routine because who wants to hear about what is going on in your life, better yet? Who cares? In the psychological world of therapy and communication, we say that individuals who don't express their feelings about what is happening are "stuffers of their feelings." We see this trait in individuals with responsibilities that supersede the world's weight on their shoulders.

Today, there are plenty of "Great Pretenders." Pretending that life is great and moving on from day to day. Making things happen to ensure that their families are more than adequately taking care of and completing the job at work with high performance. Friends are beyond ecstatic with the relationship exchange. However, spending little time to no time for yourself, playing into the false reality, you are good and all will be okay. It's time to stop pretending and take life by the horns and take complete control of what you want out of it.

"Your mental, physical, emotional, and spiritual health are counting on you to speak up and take charge."

Reflections, Thoughts, Breakthroughs

SOCIETAL ACCEPTANCE

Realizing that your best wasn't good enough in the eyes of the individuals you wanted to please can be heartbreaking.

As humans, there is this innate need for approval. It is also known as approval-seeking behavior. These behaviors stem from childhood, where children learn from their parents or guardian what is approved or disapproved behaviors in the lure of their response to one's actions displayed. These actions continue throughout each stage of life as one navigates to be accepted within the arenas of life given.

Many individuals have the urgency to feel they are a part of the "in-crowd." It reminds me of grade school antics on steroids. Adults will buy material possessions, join organizations even become affiliated with specific churches, mosques, and synagogues to show they have reached a status. What is this status that many are in search of? I like to call it the ole school keeping up with the Joneses, which I must admit, I never met them and cannot understand why so many people are hell-bent on keeping up with them.

Who are the Joneses? Where are the Joneses from? When did they establish this game so many individuals are playing or feel the need to play along? What is the end game is the question that needs to be asked to those playing along. How long do you plan to allow others to dictate you're who, what, when, where, and how?

"Is the price of being popular or fitting in worth it when you look at what you are losing by playing this game established by people you don't even know"?

Reflections, Thoughts, Breakthroughs

MENTAL HEALTH

Our psychological, social, and emotional well-being relates to our mental health. This has sparked ongoing discussion about determinants associated with mental health as the world has adhered to a complete transformation. We have observed abrupt variations and ideologies within the old mental health doctrine. What was once a taboo topic is now a household fixture that shares no means of discrimination against the masses. Yet, as the country was on lockdown during the Pandemic, people globally discovered that their psychological, social, and emotional well-being were not as solid as many would have imagined or preferred.

Our society has used the term mental health to evade, demoralize, and separate. As a therapist, I have reiterated over the years to individuals that it's okay to acknowledge and discuss any changes associated with one's well-being without fearing being labeled. Unfortunately, due to being misinformed about many determinants, many humans refused to acknowledge the changes needed and tried to continue with their day-to-day as though all was well.

After my study, I learned that about 20% of adults in the United States had experienced mental health illness. This number includes an influx of anxiety and depression as the Pandemic continues. There has been debate as many celebrated people announce their mental health needs to the world. With the reveal of those notable individuals has come an acceptance formulated by the masses to accept that it's okay to admit that you are not okay and require some more assistance to return to a position where your psychological, social, and emotional well-being is aligned.

"Mental health isn't a bad word, but it is something that needs to be discussed."

Reflections, Thoughts, Breakthroughs

UNCLE MONK

An array of feelings as I looked at a photograph of my mom and her remaining siblings after they lay to rest their youngest brother, my dear uncle, who I have loved and admired. Explaining the relationship between the two of us is complicated but inspirational. My family is an exciting collaboration of adults doing their best to make the best out of the cards dealt. Like any other family, we had our share of laughter and sorrow. However, there was a genuine love for one another despite the differences and conflicts shared.

The family teaches us life lessons we can pull from, incorporate, or run from to speak honestly. Our family should symbolize individuals who accept us despite our faults, flaws, and shortcomings and love us. I discovered early in life that your family can present you with a colder shoulder than the world of strangers you will encounter.

Now, my uncle experienced his share of adversity due to his lifestyle. Many, even myself, judged him before we discussed the lifestyle he chose to live. My judging was more confusing due to my age, so I sought answers to clarify my confusion and retrieve understanding. At that moment, I saw him through different lenses and understood that he was living within his purpose and fulfilling the life presented to him the best he could. My uncle was filled with love for all he encountered and would give you the shirt on his back. His soul was warm and welcoming. He forever perpetually words of encouragement, solidifying his pride in me and my accomplishments.

I am grateful to have had every moment we shared and embraced our time together just ten months before he transitioned. Make peace with those that you love before it's too late to do so. You will discover that you may not recall what kept you astray because it is unimportant when it's all said and done.

"Rest easy knowing you made a difference in the life of someone who poured that same energy into you out of love and respect."

Reflections, Thoughts, Breakthroughs

RUNNING

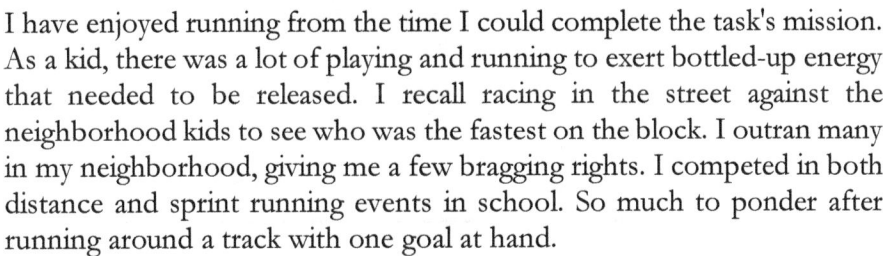

I have enjoyed running from the time I could complete the task's mission. As a kid, there was a lot of playing and running to exert bottled-up energy that needed to be released. I recall racing in the street against the neighborhood kids to see who was the fastest on the block. I outran many in my neighborhood, giving me a few bragging rights. I competed in both distance and sprint running events in school. So much to ponder after running around a track with one goal at hand.

I must admit that when we explore running from the concept of fleeing people, places, and things that no longer serve our highest good, the excitement I once felt as a kid associated with running was replaced with anxiety, nervousness, uncertainty, and fear.

Running has been a go-to for many when we are uncertain and unable to face a situation head-on. I have run from multiple concerns, only to discover that I had to return to the situation and address it no matter how uncomfortable it was to progress toward the next mission.

Our ability to step up to the circumstances and concerns presented without anxiety, nervousness, uncertainty, or fear is the mission accomplished, and the award you receive is completion.

"Running the show with the completed mission."

Reflections, Thoughts, Breakthroughs

MESSAGES

We live in a world where we are surrounded by messages. These messages we may hear, touch, see, taste, or smell play an essential role in our belief system. Do you believe everything that you have undergone with these senses?

As we hold onto a belief system, we learn and mistrust those that don't align with what we mastered. Many individuals are conflicted when they can discern the side of both systems. For example, I have experienced many symbolic messages over this lifetime. I have related to the beliefs of those individuals outside the model of what I was taught as a youth.

The question faced is, are you willing to be open to the messages presented or discredit them because you don't believe in messages? Being transparent as we live and learning to navigate our senses and beliefs can become a struggle for many. At the early onset of learning my gifts within the helping profession as a social worker, I would receive gut instincts with an essential decision about an individual's or family's well-being. My gut has never stirred me down the wrong path. However, I have gone astray down the wrong path by ignoring those gut instincts provided on several occasions.

It is vital to be in tune with all your surroundings, acknowledging any changes within those five senses provided. It's astonishing how one or more senses become heightened when another sense is lost. However, we adamantly avoid messages provided by those senses often. The symbolic connection to the messages provided is essential. Once we align with our senses to acknowledge the connection, we reach mastery within our visual, tactile, and aura dimensions.

"Messages come in all forms; being open to them is up to you."

Reflections, Thoughts, Breakthroughs

TRANSITIONS AND TRANSFORMATIONS

Several emotions erupted as I perused social media, enjoying the photographic and video memories of graduations, proms, and the welcoming of sons and daughters into our beloved sororities and fraternities. Coming in and out of life transitions can exuberate; I have experienced a spectrum of highs and lows during this recent transition. Escaping the prior transition was tumultuous. If I could simultaneously describe it, there was disorder, turmoil, indecisiveness, and a sense of unknowing. I failed a few titles and sometimes thought I had lost my sanity or at least some of it; then, my son revealed that he no longer wanted to go to college but pursue another path without genuinely knowing what path he would seek.

There was no initial shock because somewhere deep within, I knew. However, I needed to support my son while discovering how to be there for myself during this transition of life experience. The intertwining of our transitions in life was both dark and light at the same time, pushing us both to look deep within to clarify what was needed to move forth on this journey called life.

As clarification came in small increments, I understood that the comfort zone of life we take for granted was now being pulled away to allow purpose and destiny to be presented. Understand that the divine plan for pursuit overrides our personal goals.

Through it all, there was time to celebrate and give gratitude for all that took place during this season of transition and transformation. With great honor, I exclaim that I am the proud mother of a rebirthed King who completed boot camp and school to become a sailor for the United States Navy.

There are no words to describe my proud mom moment as I saw from a front-row seat the transformation of my son defeating and conquering odds trying to defeat him.

"In full declaration after undergoing a cultivating transformative transition of life."

Reflections, Thoughts, Breakthroughs

PEACE

Since I was a little girl, I have loved wearing the peace sign, which derives from being a 60s baby. I am here many decades later, still drawn to the peace sign. My sorority sister presented me with a peace sign-themed gift basket. The gesture taken and the details placed into the gift were beyond phenomenal. It meant so very much.

Today, as I reflect on the sign that represents peace, I think about the peace we require internally and externally to move about throughout the day. "Freedom from disturbance; tranquility" is the definition provided for peace. It is imperative to find peace within and understand that the peace you seek doesn't come from another. The peace you uncover and discover within will provide you with the internal and external purification you seek.

Allow the balance of your energies to remain peaceful and joyous with kindheartedness. Your thoughts should have peace, your coming and going should be with peace, your words should lead with peace, and there should be peace within your understanding of what surrounds you.

"Peace received and peace given."

Reflections, Thoughts, Breakthroughs

VULNERABILITY

During this lifetime, individuals have found themselves unable to be vulnerable due to some societal code advising that it is unacceptable. Not sure who put this code of conduct into play and why many have yet to discover that it has prevented many from moving forward.

I first learned that being vulnerable and/or revealing my vulnerability would allow individuals to ridicule or feel they had one up on me. This came from trusting the wrong individuals with some particularly personal information, only to have it repeated and used against me. I felt betrayed, yet, deep down, I knew somebody needed to hear my story as they may encounter the same and needed to know that this would pass.

When I think of the people I entrusted with my moments of vulnerability, I am grateful for their betrayal because it taught me valuable lessons. I had to work on discovering this conclusion, as those shared moments affected how I was perceived. But understanding it was all a part of the journey I needed to travel to reach the following path of understanding and clarity.

I have taken a chance on others with vulnerable moments, some have succeeded, and others have not. However, I have concluded that the information shared was placed into the universe to be used by all parties involved and that free will allows individuals their discretion. Each of us has a vulnerability threshold, and you should know what that is for you and move forward. Allow no one to make you feel you are not worthy.

"It's up to you what you share on your terms."

Reflections, Thoughts, Breakthroughs

WHY

One of the first words kids seem to learn right after the word no is why. Why can it be the sum of many things when we dissect its true meaning? For what reason or purpose has been the definition for the word; however, asking why oneself certainly provides a new perspective. It is said that the average person asks themselves up to 75 questions daily. How many of those questions consist of the word why? Looking at this day, how many whys have you presented to yourself alone, plus those surrounding you?

Analyzing from both a motivational and a critical perspective when it's explored personally. We question our motives, thoughts, clothing, food choices, vehicles, employment, relationships, and careers. So how can you rephrase those why's within your current situation and use them as motivation and inspiration to make the transformations and retrieve the clarification you require internally and externally? The answers to those motivations and inspirations lie within and are awaiting introduction.

"So many answers revealed in the whys of life."

Reflections, Thoughts, Breakthroughs

HER NEIKO

The mission of the Great Lakes trip was to celebrate my "son" shine, scheduled to graduate boot camp from the US Navy. However, a change of plans orchestrated by the universe took precedence. So I explored the city and spent quality time with someone I have loved for the last 25 years. As I think about our time over the three days, it was beyond rewarding. As I reflect on all that occurred during our time together, divine timing sums up the exchange we shared. I inherited this person I have loved over the past 25 years through marriage and gained a daughter. Oh, the things we have shared and experienced over the years. I have enjoyed many monumental occasions with my daughter: watching her ride a bike, playing sports, going to the hairdresser, prom, college, entering the US Navy, marriage, recipes, babies, purchasing a home, and becoming an incredible adult.

At the beginning of our relationship, I was so frightened that I would not meet her expectations of me as a bonus momma. I recall taking her to dinner and explaining that I was not here to take over her mom's role but to be her bonus mom or, as she likes to call me, "her Neiko." I have done my best to emulate being the best "her Neiko" that I could be for her. However, I was frightened as the relationship between her father and me ended. I did not want to lose the relationship she and I shared, but I also understood that the choice would be hers when it was all said and done.

Exploring Great Lakes was a few pieces of the life puzzle I needed to place understanding on the new journey I am navigating. You provided ample support as I revisited who and what I was in my new role to her as an adult. Thank you for our three days of exploring life on another spectrum of our relationship exchange. I love you to the moon and back and am honored to be in your life.

"Loved unconditionally without effort."

Reflections, Thoughts, Breakthroughs

MIND, BODY, SPIRIT

The focus of life has evolved over the last year to include uplifting and taking care of the elements of mind, body, and spirit. What are you doing to uplift and nurture your mind, body, and spirit? Everyone's practice will be different, but you must feed these elements of self to grow inwardly and outwardly—scientific documentation acknowledging that the mind, body, and soul must be aligned to ensure optimal well-being.

With our mind, we know that it's constantly on overdrive based on how we push it daily. That war is internal as we fight with our inner thoughts. The mind is our consciousness, so the mind needs to be renewed and transformed to align with the body and soul to create individualized well-being.

Our bodies are our temples. However, some shortcomings are associated with caring for these temples due to some miseducation along the journey. We do better when we know better; I have heard words of wisdom repeated. Although, we occasionally accommodate to avoid adhering to what we must address. It's easier said than done when you must be transparent and take responsibility for your actions.

Our soul and spirit are defined separately within a religious, spiritual, and nonreligious doctrine platform. Is it essential to understand how your soul or spirit collaborates with you? Are you being attentive to the signs provided? Our soul flourishes when aligned with our mind and body awareness. The three working together in harmony is the quintessence of our journey.

"The alignment of these three provides great input and output within our journey."

Reflections, Thoughts, Breakthroughs

DEBRA FAYE

When carried within your mother's womb, you bring forth the powers of multiple generations within. Regarding the generations of men and women embedded within the fiber of my being, I like to describe them as mystical in many words yet powerful on many levels.

Within the last few years, I have had the opportunity to ask, seek and reflect on some family narratives, genes, and attributes that were important for some releasing and healing. As I started to rediscover and define who I was, I knew deep within that I would need help to answer questions to obtain clarification.

My mother has always been open to answering questions supplied. However, these questions and inquiries required her to be vulnerable and present a side of her that I had never seen truly up close and personal. You see, my mother, the steel exterior she presents was formed out of adversity, hardship, mistrust, and environmental circumstance. Although the exterior was formed of steel, there have been glimpses of a more loving, tender interior as I have gotten older and see her story through her eyes. It is essential to understand that each of us is shaped by some circumstances that either we can move past or continue to harbor because we are not sure how to move on from those situations associated with the circumstances.

Having an opportunity to acquire, listen and ponder on the stories associated with the woman that gave me life gave me a more explicit interpretation of the woman I call momma. I am reminded that I come from strength and perseverance despite the barriers.

So when I have not met the mark and am uncertain of the next move, I am confident in moving forward, knowing I have what it takes to fulfill my pursuits and aspirations. Do you know why? Because that woman of steel I call momma provided me with what it takes to take on life and make the best of it. For that and much more, I thank you for life and all the sacrifices to ensure I live in my purpose and make you and our ancestors proud.

"Thank you, Momma, for it all, even when I did not understand the lessons within the lessons."

Reflections, Thoughts, Breakthroughs

RELEASING AND HEALING

Releasing and healing come hand in hand, and we should not suppress either. Be honest with yourself on what needs to be released as you seek the healing to move forward into your authentic self-journey. If I am being transparent, I have doubted many of my decisions due to them positioning me in an uncomfortable position with myself and taking responsibility for my actions. To truly heal, you must forgive. It begins with forgiving yourself and others you have allowed to violate your time, space, and energy. An enormous pill to swallow as I prepared for my journey of healing and forgiving.

Uncovering when it's time to love again is a complex equation. You must first have unconditional love for yourself before exploring any authentic relational love. I have consistently been in long-term relationships, and for the first time in my adult life, I am not in a relationship nor seeking to secure one. So although it might be regaling to have some companionship, it isn't straightforward and comes with soul-searching questions.

Studies have proven that most humans will leap into a new relationship without providing adequate time to process and heal from their previous relationship. So acquiring to know who you are coming out of a relationship and entering a new one is paramount.

I am not the woman I was entering this new journey; I am a much better version of myself with greater insight than I envisioned. I appreciate every learning lesson and discovery upon this awakened journey of self as I embark upon a new seasoned version of myself in my mid-fifties. Reencountering love again during this lifetime may or may not occur; however, discovering a new love for myself and knowing what I will not accept is golden.

"To thyself be true, and all else will follow."

Reflections, Thoughts, Breakthroughs

BROTHERS AND SISTERS

I discovered that individuals are placed on our paths for lessons to be solved and growth to be established on many levels. I was once told that I would be introduced to my brothers and sisters of the light and that I would know who they were when I encountered them. Internally, I thought, who precisely will these individuals be placed into my life at such a fragile stage. I have had the opportunity to meet some phenomenal humans with their own junctures of fragility. Many I could relate to due to the parallel correlations that bond us and others. I needed to trust there was a reason behind the lesson of our paths crossing. Was it time to convey some of my most prominent fears, hurts, and pains with strangers' season, or was I to be there with a listening ear to provide emotional support during their fragile moments? I admit I did not know the correct answer; however, in each encounter, the answers were presented, and I was being propelled to come outside of my comfort zone using the gifts bestowed upon me during an emotional path of discovery and healing of self.

During this season of meeting my brothers and sisters of the lights, I was transparent on many levels to ensure that what each of them needed from me on their path was provided. Understanding that some will cross your path for a word of encouragement is essential, while others may require more intense indoctrination. I discovered that some I encountered during this season were simply for me to be in the presence of their gifts, allowing me to accept what I required of them during this time of being present. We all have something unique to offer one another; however, at times, we aren't ready to accept or give those gifts due to our inability to accept the role expected from each of us. Simply to be brothers and sisters of the light and be there for one another when we need our lights to be restored with love.

"We each have a shining light that will require restoration at some point in this lifetime, be open to the individual or individuals that have been sent to carry out the mission."

Reflections, Thoughts, Breakthroughs

SEASONAL

Everything within this life has its season. Many fruits and vegetables are seasonal, and although we can find or locate them outside their regular season, we can expect to pay more or find that the flavor differs from when it's within its season. I have discovered that we as humans have seasonal obstacles, pains, heartaches, transformations, and transitions we must undergo in this life. I call them seasonal because, with the growth, we step into new seasons, and we all know that within a growing season, there will be obstacles, pains, heartaches, transformation, and transitions. Over the years, I have discovered that individuals can also fall into this seasonal category. I call them seasonal family members, friends, and associates. I identified that my definition of family and friends does not equate to those I once considered within the category of such; however, I later discovered that they were simply seasonal in their role. I am exceptionally grateful for each season I experience and look forward to many more.

"Identifying your season allows your transition to be somewhat smoother."

Reflections, Thoughts, Breakthroughs

STARTING SOMETHING NEW

Starting something new by choice or force will create an array of psychological biases. The theory of starting anew must be analyzed to adequately concede the required input and output. When we introduce something new, we immediately process the results envisioned subconsciously.

Unfortunately, life has a way of placing mirages upon our envisioned outcome. Mentally, when we cannot favorably complete an assignment or task rendered, we classify privately as failures based on society's input and inner self.

I recall preparing for my licensure examination, and upon my first attempt, I came up way short and left the testing center feeling defeated, thinking, what now. I can either give up or keep going at this thing until I receive the outcome I endeavor to acquire. After testing anxiety and negative chatter, I settled on the latter and eventually received the passing score required. During that encounter and several others I have lived through, I learned that no individual can dictate your path and that timing is divine.

To prepare for completing a start over within this next phase of life, I am ecstatic and encouraged that I have the chance to update elements that were not adequately in harmony—facing the truth and returning to the assignment or task when I needed to make the improvements. However, it is imperative to recognize that when it comes to self and what is in the most significant interest of self, that self is the only one that can determine what commands a start-over moment.

You should take a moment to breathe, reflect, and know that starting over is one of the best decisions you can make for yourself. It only requires you to decide what you want for yourself now.

"Starting over is everything because I said so."

Reflections, Thoughts, Breakthroughs

A NEW MEANING OF LOVE

Today as I watch from afar, enjoying the European scenery of brunch at a café, love is definitely in the air. However, the love I am seeing is associated with self-love. I have had the opportunity to explore and define love from many perspectives during this lifetime. However, I have discovered that I needed to look within and redefine the true meaning of love. The word itself means so much more to me from various stances.

My once hopeless romantic reference to self has been redefined regarding love and placing a meaning upon the word in general. Learning not to place unimaginable expectations upon something that was not to be complicated was my conclusion, as I had mislabeled the meaning by simply placing love into a paradigm of all things romantic.

How to love and be loved from many life experiences has provided a misconception of love in general for society. Here are a few questions we should contemplate regarding love, when do we define love for ourselves without the judgment and ridicule of others? Should we allow others to define how we love ourselves or others, or should we go about love freely, understanding that life is about love when it's all said and done? We all should find love within first to project love externally for those in need.

"You define love, and your love is everything to this world."

Reflections, Thoughts, Breakthroughs

REINTRODUCTION

We live in a culture where a brief review of self is expected through a casual conversation, attending a class for the first time, a conference/seminar, and job interviews. I have often deliberated what I would say to describe myself, using precise words to capture the attention of those standing by listening. The fear of coming across as dull habitually crisscrossed my subconscious because everyone else invariably produces excellent intros. On the flip side of reflecting on what I would say, I often queried who am I? For decades, I contemplated who I am and what my gifts are.

I have often said that I am a country girl from Nashville, Tennessee, being my authentic self as my representation of self. Not secure with knowing my true gifts to the world. I have had the distinct honor of keeping several titles and wearing many hats, including daughter, sister, aunt, soror, friend, lover, girlfriend, wife, mother, grandmother, social worker, counselor, coworker, professor, and board member. I most recently went from a wife to a divorcee. A mother that no longer felt needed nor had the answers to soothe, and a daughter that had to stand up for herself respectfully and claim ownership of herself as a woman with boundaries. These modifications required me to reach deep within and examine who I am now. Being straightforward with the person staring at me in the mirror and applying my advice furnished to friends, family, and clients over the years into actions if I took complete ownership of myself and what I represented and owned it.

I am a woman bent but not broken, although I often felt like I had been broken into many pieces due to the obstacles and circumstances confronting me through many seasons. I often relive the traumatic feelings of insecurity and not being enough. Through the internalization of those feelings, I discovered a new journey. This journey led me to acknowledge my faults and flaws and take ownership of the gifts bestowed upon me. See, I have flaws and take full responsibility for those flaws that have played into some not-so-good moments. However, I have exceptional gifts and had to take full accountability for them. Thus, acknowledge that God has given me gifts I intend to use and not lose. I recall being told you would lose something if you didn't use it. We are made uniquely so and perfect in the eyes of our creator, each provided with our specific gifts. I call my gifts my special powers specifically created for me.

Each individual's journey will be different because we each have something to be discovered within this life to fulfill our destinies. I have learned that you cannot compare yourself to others or their blessings because their path is theirs and not for you to analyze. Your role in this motion picture called life is to enjoy it to the fullest. Amplify and use your superpowers, being your authentic self and owning it. Sharing those gifts provided and walking in them confidently, knowing they were individually scribed and created for you.

Be mindful that our visions will change throughout the seasons. It's associated with our growth. Let me introduce myself; I am Roneiko Daniele Henderson, co-creator of the establishment of me, myself, and I. Sharing my gifts/superpowers bestowed upon me by the master creator of my life, walking fearless and confidently, knowing I am covered and armored, embracing this life and all opportunities provided. I share my gift as a helper, encouraging, inspiring, and motivating those whose path I cross with truth and love. My gifts are many, used when required. And I am exceedingly grateful for each.

"Reintroductions are great; they let people know who they are encountering."

Reflections, Thoughts, Breakthroughs

www.ingramcontent.com/pod-product-compliance
Lightning Source LLC
Chambersburg PA
CBHW072150200426
43209CB00051B/1085